Early praise for *Automate with Grunt*

Whether you're still writing your first Grunt task or trying to come up with a complex workflow, this compact and pragmatic book will prove to be a handy companion and give you the confidence to explore the full and rich Grunt ecosystem.

➤ **Peter Cooper**
Managing editor, JavaScript Weekly

This book focuses on how Grunt works and not on the "just do this; just do that" steps that you typically see in blog posts and documentation. Brian quickly and effectively shows how to integrate Grunt into your own workflow and how to customize your workflow for ultimate web-development productivity.

➤ **Jenna Pederson**
Independent developer, 612 Software Foundry

I've spent countless hours working with Grunt to build a developer tool called Lineman. Unfortunately, Grunt's documentation alone was never enough to show me the simplest, most conventional way to accomplish what I needed. If I'd had this book to help me back when I first started, I would have established a deeper, meaningful understanding of Grunt much more quickly!

➤ **Justin Searls**
Co-Founder, Test Double, LLC

This book is a quick and easy dive into a task-running tool whose power and simplicity are surprising. The examples in this book are fun to follow and also incredibly practical for any developer.

➤ **Jessica Janiuk**
Front-end developer

Automate with Grunt

The Build Tool for JavaScript

Brian P. Hogan

The Pragmatic Bookshelf

Dallas, Texas • Raleigh, North Carolina

Many of the designations used by manufacturers and sellers to distinguish their products are claimed as trademarks. Where those designations appear in this book, and The Pragmatic Programmers, LLC was aware of a trademark claim, the designations have been printed in initial capital letters or in all capitals. The Pragmatic Starter Kit, The Pragmatic Programmer, Pragmatic Programming, Pragmatic Bookshelf, PragProg and the linking *g* device are trademarks of The Pragmatic Programmers, LLC.

Every precaution was taken in the preparation of this book. However, the publisher assumes no responsibility for errors or omissions, or for damages that may result from the use of information (including program listings) contained herein.

Our Pragmatic courses, workshops, and other products can help you and your team create better software and have more fun. For more information, as well as the latest Pragmatic titles, please visit us at *http://pragprog.com*.

The team that produced this book includes:

Susannah Davidson Pfalzer (editor)
Candace Cunningham (copyeditor)
David J Kelly (typesetter)
Janet Furlow (producer)
Ellie Callahan (support)

For international rights, please contact *rights@pragprog.com*.

Printed in the United States of America.
ISBN-13: 9781941222119
Printed on acid-free paper.
Book version: P1.0—April 2014

Contents

Acknowledgments

First, thank you for picking up this book. I wrote it because I was frustrated at the lack of meaningful Grunt documentation online. Hopefully you find this a nice, handy quick start.

Next, The Pragmatic Bookshelf continues to be the absolute best place to publish books. Dave Thomas and Andy Hunt always provide just the right amount of guidance, and my wonderful editor Susannah Pfalzer once again made sure that everything I wanted to say actually made sense.

The technical reviewers for this book were excellent and thorough, trying every example to find out what worked and what didn't, and keeping me honest when it came to explaining how things functioned. Thank you, Andrea Barisone, Kevin Beam, Daniel Bretoi, Trevor Burnham, Alex Henry, Jeff Holland, Jessica Janiuk, Jenna Pederson, Stephen Orr, and Justin Searls, for all of your great feedback and insights along the way.

Thanks to my business associates Chris Warren, Chris Johnson, Mike Weber, Nick LaMuro, Austen Ott, Erich Tesky, Kevin Gisi, Jon Kinney, and Myles Steinhauser for their continued support.

Finally, thank you, Carissa, Ana, and Lisa, for your love, understanding, and support. And for being awesome.

Preface

Web development has changed. The days of opening a few text files in your editor of choice and then uploading them to the live site are long gone. Today's web applications demand complex styling and functionality that only advanced CSS and JavaScript can provide. These assets get quite large and unwieldy, and the process requires a new workflow.

The JavaScript community has embraced Grunt, a powerful automation tool and task runner written in JavaScript, to handle these workflows. With Grunt, you can watch files for changes, concatenate CSS files and JavaScript files together, obfuscate or minify client-side code, run tests, and check your code for syntax errors, all automatically. Unfortunately, a lot of documentation on Grunt centers on copying and pasting various bits of code rather than focusing on how Grunt itself works.

This book will help you understand how Grunt works and show you how you can make it part of your development process. When you're done you'll be able to use Grunt on your own projects and build your own tasks and plug-ins.

What's in This Book

This guide is meant to be a quick overview of Grunt, using hands-on examples to illustrate its features.

We'll start out by looking at the very basics of Grunt, defining some simple tasks as we build our first Gruntfile. We'll create basic tasks, create tasks that take in parameters, chain tasks together, and document tasks. Then we'll look at Grunt's built-in tools for working with files and folders on the file system.

After that we'll look at multitasks, a feature of Grunt that lets us define a single task that can have multiple output targets. This is useful for file conversion and other tasks where you might need to create separate distributions from a single source.

Next we'll use several Grunt plug-ins together as we configure a workflow to develop a modern single-page web application with CoffeeScript and the AngularJS framework. We'll cover conversion, minification, and file watching so you can see how easy Grunt makes automating important repetitive tasks.

Then we'll look at what it takes to create our very own plug-in for Grunt. This will give us a chance to explore how Grunt can leverage Node.js and external programs, as well as how to break Grunt tasks into reusable modules.

And finally, we'll use Grunt to create project scaffolds. We'll play with existing plug-ins and then we'll create our very own project template that we can use when we start our own web projects.

In addition, each chapter gives you suggestions for further exploration, offering you the opportunity to dig deeper into Grunt.

Who Should Read This Book

If you're a web developer working with CSS and JavaScript and you've never used Grunt, you need this book. Grunt's features can make your workflow so much easier to manage. If your only experience with Grunt is copying and pasting some lines of configuration, you'll find value here, as well. Grunt has become a standard for JavaScript projects on both the client and the server. Knowing how it works will be incredibly valuable.

This book assumes that you know some basic programming and that you're not afraid to write JavaScript code. The Grunt tasks we use will be written in JavaScript using Node.js.

What You Need

You'll need a computer running Windows 7 or 8 or a modern version of Linux or OS X. You'll need the ability to install software on your computer, as well as an active Internet connection.

You'll also need a text editor or your IDE of choice. You can use Sublime Text, which is a commercial editor with a trial period, or any other text editor that you'd write code in.[1]

We'll use Node.js, so you'll need to visit the Node.js website and get the latest version installed.[2] You'll find installers for all platforms there. Download the one for your operating system and install it using the default options.

---

1. http://www.sublimetext.com/
2. http://nodejs.org

Finally, Grunt is a command-line utility, so you'll use the Command Prompt on Windows or the Terminal on OS X or Linux. This book will guide you through that process, so you'll be pretty comfortable by the end. If you're used to graphical programs, it might seem a bit shocking to you that you have to go "old school," but a lot of modern developers use command-line tools because of the flexibility they offer. You'll run Grunt on the command line, but you'll still use your normal workflow and tools to write your apps.

Conventions

As you work through the book, you'll see some conventions.

When you're asked to type a command in the Command Prompt or Terminal, which I'll just refer to as the Terminal, it'll look like this:

```
$ grunt
```

The dollar sign ($) represents the prompt in your Terminal. You never type that part of the command. But when you see it, that means you will need to type the command in your Terminal.

Sometimes you'll see snippets of code you'll type out. Those will look like this:

basics/kicking_tires/Gruntfile.js
```
module.exports = function(grunt){
  // Your tasks go here
}
```

The filename above the code indicates the file we're working with. You can use this to locate the full file in the book's source code download, too. And if you're reading the electronic copy of the book, you can click or tap on the name of the file to view the file online.

Sometimes you'll see output from the screen, which will look like this:

```
Available tasks
       default  Custom task.
         greet  Custom task.
    addNumbers  Custom task.
           all  Alias for "default", "greet:Brian", "addNumbers:2:3" tasks.
        praise  Have Grunt say nice things about you.
```

This is a hands-on book, so there will be many places where we'll reference files or commands. The book's formatting should make it clear which file or command you're expected to work with.

Where to Go for Help

The book's web page contains a link to the book's forum, where you can ask questions and provide feedback.[3] When reporting any problems, please be sure to report the version of the book you're reading.

And now, with all that out of the way, let's dig into how Grunt works.

---

3. http://pragprog.com/book/bhgrunt/

CHAPTER 1

The Very Basics

Grunt is a task runner, designed to be more configuration than code. And while many of the examples you'll see in the wild involve copying and pasting configuration snippets and loading plug-ins, don't be fooled into thinking that's all Grunt can do. Sure, there are some amazing plug-ins that will vastly improve your workflow, but if you know JavaScript, Grunt becomes a very powerful automation tool for many types of projects. If you have a manual repetitive task you run as part of your development or deployment process, chances are there's a way to automate that process with Grunt.

In this chapter we'll set up our first project with Grunt and cover how the basic task system works. We'll use simple JavaScript programs to highlight and explore Grunt's basic features. By the end you'll be able to create basic tasks and handle errors.

Installing Grunt and Configuring a Gruntfile

Before we can do anything with Grunt, we have to install the Grunt command-line tool. Grunt is written in Node.js, and to install it we use npm, the tool Node uses to download and manage dependencies. Open a new Terminal and type the following command:

```
$ npm install -g grunt-cli
```

This installs the Grunt command-line utility globally. On Linux or OS X, you may need to run this command using sudo if you get a "Permission Denied" error.

Grunt is broken into separate packages, each serving a specific purpose. The grunt-cli package gives us a command-line interface. But to use this interface, we have to install the grunt package as well; installing grunt-cli doesn't automatically install grunt for us.

Instead, we install Grunt into our project as a dependency. The grunt-cli tool we installed globally on our system will then work with the version of grunt within our project. Let's create a simple project folder and set everything up.

Create a new folder called kicking_tires and navigate into that folder in your Terminal:

```
$ mkdir kicking_tires
$ cd kicking_tires
```

From here, you could install Grunt with npm install grunt, but there's a better way. Node.js applications use a file called package.json to store the metadata about a project as well as track a project's dependencies. If we create this file, we can add Grunt as a dependency to our project, making it easier to set things up in the future.

Type the following command to create a new package.json file.

```
$ npm init
```

You'll be asked a series of questions about your project. For this project you can leave everything at the default settings. Your package.json file will end up looking like this when the wizard finishes:

```
{
  "name": "kicking_tires",
  "version": "0.0.0",
  "description": "",
  "main": "index.js",
  "scripts": {
    "test": "echo \"Error: no test specified\" &amp;&amp; exit 1"
  },
  "author": "",
  "license": "BSD-2-Clause"
}
```

Now that we have this file in place, we can add Grunt as a development dependency like this:

```
$ npm install grunt --save-dev
```

Grunt will be installed into the node_modules/ subfolder of the current folder, and it'll be added to the package.json file as a development dependency. If you look at your package.json file you'll see this at the bottom now:

```
"devDependencies": {
  "grunt": "~0.4.4"
}
```

The devDependencies section lists dependencies that are used only to build an application. Grunt isn't something an application needs to run; we use Grunt only as a tool for developing an application. However, a library that lets us connect to a MySQL database would be a true dependency, not a development dependency.

The --save-dev command also saves the version number into the package.json file, and it uses the tilde in front of the version number to signify that any version 0.4.4 or higher is OK for us to use. Version 0.4.7, for example, would be valid, but 0.5.0 would not. This helps us stay current within minor version numbers, but prevents us from accidentally installing a version that's too new and incompatible. Of course, we can change this version number by hand if we like.

The node_modules folder contains all of the libraries our project depends on. This means you have a copy of the Grunt library itself in the node_modules folder.

Adding things as development dependencies allows new people who want to work on our project to easily download all of the dependencies we specify by issuing the npm install command in the folder that contains the package.json file. In fact, let's try this now. Remove the node_modules folder and then run npm install. You'll see that npm fetches Grunt again, creating a new node_modules folder.

With Grunt installed, we can test things out by running it from the command line:

```
$ grunt
```

This fires off the grunt-cli library we installed globally, which then uses the grunt library we installed in our project's node_modules folder. This lets us easily use different versions of Grunt on different projects.

But when we look at our output, we see this message:

```
A valid Gruntfile could not be found. Please see the getting started guide for
more information on how to configure grunt: http://gruntjs.com/getting-started
Fatal error: Unable to find Gruntfile.
```

Grunt is telling us that we need something called a Gruntfile in our project. A Gruntfile is a JavaScript file that specifies and configures the tasks you want to be able to run for your project. It's like a Makefile. Grunt is specifically looking for a file called Gruntfile.js in the current working directory and it can't find one, so it doesn't know what we want it to do. Let's create a Gruntfile.

Our First Task

Let's kick the tires. We'll create the default task, which is the one that runs when we type the grunt command.

Every Gruntfile starts out with some boilerplate code. Create a new file called Gruntfile.js and add this:

```
basics/kicking_tires/Gruntfile.js
module.exports = function(grunt){
  // Your tasks go here
}
```

If you're familiar with Node.js and its module system, you'll understand what's going on here. If you're not, it's not a huge deal; just know that this is what Grunt needs to interpret your tasks. You're defining a Node.js module that receives a grunt object. You'll use that object and its methods throughout your configuration files. The tasks you define and configure are then made available to Grunt so that they can be executed.

Now, within the curly braces, define the following task, which prints some text to the screen:

```
basics/kicking_tires/Gruntfile.js
grunt.registerTask('default', function(){
  console.log('Hello from Grunt.');
});
```

We use grunt.registerTask() to create a new Grunt task. We pass in a task name followed by an associated callback function. Whatever we put in the callback function is executed when we invoke the task.

To see it in action, run this new task from the Terminal:

```
$ grunt
```

You'll see the following output:

```
Running "default" task
Hello from Grunt.

Done, without errors.
```

In this task we've used Node's console.log function, but we really should use Grunt's grunt.log() object instead. It'll give us some flexibility because it supports error logging, warnings, and other handy features.

So, change the following:

`basics/kicking_tires/Gruntfile.js`
```
console.log('Hello from Grunt.');
```

to

`basics/kicking_tires/Gruntfile.js`
```
grunt.log.writeln('Hello from Grunt.');
```

and rerun the task with

```
$ grunt
```

You shouldn't see anything different. This task is not fancy by any means, but it illustrates that Grunt works, and that we can create a simple task. Let's move on.

Handling Parameters

Grunt task definitions can take in simple arguments. Let's demonstrate how this works by creating a simple "greeting" task. As before, we'll use grunt.registerTask() to create a task, but this time we'll define a parameter in the callback function.

`basics/kicking_tires/Gruntfile.js`
```
grunt.registerTask('greet', function(name){
  grunt.log.writeln('Hi there, ' + name);
});
```

In the body of the callback, we reference the variable just like we would in any plain JavaScript code.

Run this task with

```
$ grunt greet
```

and you'll see this output:

```
Running "greet" task
Hi there, undefined

Done, without errors.
```

We didn't actually pass an argument to the task, and so the `name` parameter's value is undefined. Grunt didn't throw an error message at us.

To supply the parameter, we use a colon followed by the value, like this:

```
$ grunt greet:Brian
```

And now we see what we're looking for.

```
Running "greet:Brian" (greet) task
Hi there, Brian
```

```
Done, without errors.
```

We don't have to stop at one argument, though. We can define tasks with multiple arguments. Let's create another rather silly task that adds some numbers together.

In the Gruntfile, add this task:

basics/kicking_tires/Gruntfile.js
```
grunt.registerTask('addNumbers', function(first, second){
  var answer = Number(first) + Number(second);
  grunt.log.writeln(first + ' + ' + second + ' is ' + answer);
});
```

To run this task, we have to supply both numbers as arguments to the task, and we do that using colons, like this:

$ grunt addNumbers:1:2

And when we do that, we see this result:

```
Running "addNumbers:1:2" (addNumbers) task
1 + 2 is 3
```

```
Done, without errors.
```

Pretty easy so far, isn't it? But what if the user didn't enter appropriate values? We need a way to handle that gracefully.

Throwing Errors

When things go wrong in our tasks, we'll want to log error messages. We can do that with grunt.log().

In our addNumbers() task, let's check to make sure the first argument is a number. If it isn't, we'll print an error on the screen:

basics/kicking_tires/Gruntfile.js
```
if(isNaN(Number(first))){
  grunt.warn('The first argument must be a number.');
}
```

Now run this with

$ grunt addNumbers:a:2

and you'll see an interesting response from Grunt:

```
Running "addNumbers:a:2" (addNumbers) task
Warning: The first argument must be a number. Use --force to continue.
```

Grunt prints out our message and then stops the task. It doesn't attempt to do the math. However, it tells us that we can force it to continue by running our task with the --force option. Let's try that:

```
$ grunt addNumbers:a:2 --force
Running "addNumbers:a:2" (addNumbers) task
Warning: The first argument must be a number. Used --force, continuing.
a + 2 is NaN

Done, but with warnings.
```

We still see the warning, but the task continues. Sometimes we need to allow users to be able to force their way through tasks that don't work. However, you can prevent people from doing this by using grunt.fatal() instead.

We've defined a few tasks in our file, but what if we wanted to invoke all of these tasks at once?

Chaining Tasks

So far we haven't done anything with Grunt that we couldn't do with Bash, PowerShell, Perl, Python, or any other scripting language. But Grunt offers the ability to create one task that fires off other tasks. Grunt refers to this as an alias.

To make a task like this we use registerTask() and pass it an array of tasks instead of a callback function.

```
basics/kicking_tires/Gruntfile.js
grunt.registerTask('all', ['default', 'greet:Brian', 'addNumbers:2:3']);
```

Notice that when we do this we pass these task names as strings, which means we can pass arguments as well.

We've called this task all, but if we renamed it to default we'd be able to run this task by running grunt with no arguments. The default task is commonly used to run the test suite for a project.

Now let's look at one more basic but really important piece: adding a little documentation to our tasks.

Describing Tasks

So far, we've defined a Grunt task using two arguments: a name and a callback function, or a name and an array of tasks that we want to call. But the registerTask() method can take three arguments. After the name, we can specify a text description of the task.

Let's define a simple task called praise() that makes Grunt say some words of encouragement to you.

```
basics/kicking_tires/Gruntfile.js
grunt.registerTask('praise',
                   'Have Grunt say nice things about you.', function(){
  var praise = [
    "You're awesome.",
    "You're the best developer ever!",
    "You are extremely attractive.",
    "Everyone loves you!"
  ]
  var pick = praise[(Math.floor(Math.random() * praise.length))];
  grunt.log.writeln(pick);

});
```

Now type this:

```
$ grunt --help
```

This shows Grunt's basic help page, but in the middle of the output you'll see this:

```
Available tasks
    default  Custom task.
      greet  Custom task.
 addNumbers  Custom task.
        all  Alias for "default", "greet:Brian", "addNumbers:2:3" tasks.
     praise  Have Grunt say nice things about you.
```

All the tasks we didn't document just say "Custom task," but our praise() task shows its description. It's really important that we document the tasks that we create so others who follow our work will know what those tasks do. As we go forward we'll be sure to do that.

If you'd like a nicer way to see your tasks, take a look at the grunt-available-tasks plug-in, which gives a simple list of the tasks that isn't buried in the help.[1]

What's Next?

In this chapter we looked at the basics of creating our own Grunt tasks, handling arguments for tasks, and adding some documentation along the way. Before moving on, try the following:

---

1. https://npmjs.org/package/grunt-available-tasks

- Add documentation to the other tasks. Be sure to test each task to make sure you got the syntax right!

- Create a new task that multiplies two numbers. Be sure to add documentation.

- Create a new folder called learning_grunt and then generate a new package.json file. Then create a new Gruntfile in the project, with a default task that prints out "It worked!"

Next we'll look at how we can use built-in Grunt utilities to work with the file system.

CHAPTER 2

Manage Files

We've spent a little time with Grunt covering the basics, but running fun little JavaScript programs doesn't really show off what Grunt can do. When you're using Grunt in one of your projects, it's very likely you'll do some work with the file system. For example, you might read some settings in from a file, or you might write your own files to disk. You might need to create files and folders or copy files around. You can do all of these things by calling out to the operating system yourself using Node.js, but Grunt provides tools to do it easily. In this chapter we'll explore those tools as we build a simple Grunt task to copy a manifest of files in our project to a working folder that we can upload to our web server.

Creating the Project

Let's create a project folder called deployment and then navigate into it:

```
$ mkdir deployment
$ cd deployment
$ npm init
```

Fill in the basic information or leave it at its default values. Alternatively, create your own package.json file that contains this:

```
{
  "name": "deploying",
  "version": "0.0.0",
  "description": "A simple project to copy files for deployment."
}
```

Next, we add Grunt as a dependency:

```
$ npm install grunt --save-dev
```

Now we'll create a basic Gruntfile.js with the following content:

```
files/simple/deploying/Gruntfile.js
module.exports = function(grunt){
}
```

Now let's create a few simple files and folders in this project. First, create an index.html file with a default HTML5 template:

```
files/simple/deploying/index.html
<!DOCTYPE html>
<html lang="en-US">
  <head>
    <meta charset="utf-8">
    <title>Test page</title>
    <link rel="stylesheet" href="stylesheets/style.css">
  </head>
  <body>
    <h1>Test page</h1>
  </body>
</html>
```

Then create the folders stylesheets and javascripts:

```
$ mkdir stylesheets
$ mkdir javascripts
```

After that, create a stylesheets/style.css file with the following contents:

```
files/simple/deploying/stylesheets/style.css
h1{color: #F00;}
```

We're not putting much in the files for this exercise; we just want some text in there so we'll know later on that the files copied correctly. If we left them blank we wouldn't be sure if the right things got copied.

Finally, create the file javascripts/app.js, which looks like this:

```
files/simple/deploying/javascripts/app.js
var app = {};
app.name = 'Hello';
```

With the setup out of the way, let's jump into how we work with these files in Grunt tasks.

Creating and Deleting Directories

For our task to copy files from their original location to a destination directory, we need to create that destination directory. And every time we want to re-create the destination folder we'll need to delete it and its contents. So let's use Grunt's built-in tools to create two tasks—one to create the folder and one to delete it.

Specifying Configuration Options

Grunt provides grunt.config.init(), which lets us define the configuration for our Grunt tasks by passing in a JavaScript object with the properties and values for our tasks.

files/simple/deploying/Gruntfile.js
```
grunt.config.init({
});
```

When you install and configure a Grunt plug-in, you'll often have to add some properties and values to this configuration object. Typically you'll add a property for the specific plug-in, and then that property will have its own configuration object.

While we're not building a plug-in here, let's follow the same approach. We'll create a property called copyFiles and place our configuration variables within that object.

A best practice for creating configuration options for a task is to place all options within an options property. This avoids any potential collision with Grunt's API.

Let's define our first option. We need a way to specify the destination folder that we'll copy our files to, so we'll create an option for the workingDirectory:

files/simple/deploying/Gruntfile.js
```
copyFiles: {
  options: {
    workingDirectory: 'working',
  }
}
```

We're going to leave a trailing comma after the value when we're writing configuration options. That way we won't forget to add it when we add a new option to this section later. However, this is not valid according to the specifications for ECMAScript 6. Grunt and Node.js won't complain, but JavaScript syntax checkers (and seasoned JavaScript developers) might. When you're done writing your configurations, you'll definitely want to remove trailing commas.

Creating a Folder

Grunt's built-in grunt.util.mkdir() method creates folders, and so all we have to do is create a task, read the name of the directory from our configuration object, and create the folder.

files/simple/deploying/Gruntfile.js
```
grunt.registerTask('createFolder', 'Create the working folder', function(){
  grunt.config.requires('copyFiles.options.workingDirectory');

  grunt.file.mkdir(grunt.config.get('copyFiles.options.workingDirectory'));
});
```

We're using grunt.config.requires() to ensure that the configuration property we want has been set. The task will abort if the field isn't specified. Notice that we can use a string with dot notation to look up properties in the configuration object. We then use grunt.config.get() to fetch the value out of the object and use it to create the folder, using the same dot notation.

At the command line we can run

```
$ grunt createFolder
```

and we'll see the new working folder in our directory.

Removing Folders

To remove the working folder, we can write a very similar task, but this time we'll use Grunt's grunt.file.delete() method instead. This deletes a file, or a folder and all of its contents.

files/simple/deploying/Gruntfile.js
```
grunt.registerTask('clean',
    'Deletes the working folder and its contents', function(){
  grunt.config.requires('copyFiles.options.workingDirectory');

  grunt.file.delete(grunt.config.get('copyFiles.options.workingDirectory'));
});
```

One of the biggest advantages of using these Grunt utilities instead of the raw operating-system commands is that they will work on multiple operating systems. The syntax for recursively deleting folders is very different between Linux and Windows.

Now let's look at how we copy the files over.

Copying Files

Our project may have lots of files that we don't want to deploy to the web server. For example, there's no need to send up our Gruntfile.js or the node_modules folder if we're building a basic website. So we'll need to tell Grunt what files we want to copy over. Let's create a new manifest property of our copyFiles configuration object, which will be an array of file paths we want to copy.

```
copyFiles: {
  options: {
    workingDirectory: 'working',
    manifest: [
      'index.html', 'stylesheets/style.css', 'javascripts/app.js'
    ]
```

Grunt provides grunt.file.copy(), which lets us specify a source file and a destination. Unlike the grunt.file.delete() method, it doesn't handle folders. We'll address that later. For now we'll just be very explicit and list every file we want in our manifest property.

Our copyFiles task will check for the workingDirectory and manifest properties and then iterate over the files in the manifest, copying each file into the working folder.

```
grunt.registerTask('copyFiles', function(){
  var files, workingDirectory;

  grunt.config.requires('copyFiles.options.manifest');
  grunt.config.requires('copyFiles.options.workingDirectory');

  files = grunt.config.get('copyFiles.options.manifest');
  workingDirectory = grunt.config.get('copyFiles.options.workingDirectory');
  files.forEach(function(file) {
    var destination = workingDirectory + '/' + file;
    grunt.log.writeln('Copying ' + file + ' to ' + destination);
    grunt.file.copy(file, destination);
  });
});
```

We can run this task with

```
$ grunt copyFiles
Running "copyFiles" task
Copying index.html to working/index.html
Copying stylesheets/style.css to working/stylesheets/style.css
Copying javascripts/app.js to working/javascripts/app.js

Done, without errors.
```

and the files are copied into our working folder.

Now, to make this all fit together nicely, let's create a new task that runs the clean, createFolder, and copyFiles tasks. Let's call the task deploy, shall we?

```
grunt.registerTask('deploy', 'Deploys files',
             ['clean', 'createFolder', 'copyFiles']);
```

Run this new task:

```
$ grunt deploy
Running "clean" task

Running "createFolder" task

Running "copyFiles" task
Copying index.html to working/index.html
Copying stylesheets/style.css to working/stylesheets/style.css
Copying javascripts/app.js to working/javascripts/app.js

Done, without errors.
```

You'll see that all of the tasks ran in the order we specified, and all of the files were copied into the working folder as expected. Technically, we don't need the createFolder task; Grunt's grunt.file.copy() will create the destination folder if it doesn't exist. But it's best to be specific.

So far we've demonstrated that we can use Grunt's built-in file tools to copy individual files, but what we've built here works only if we specify the individual files we want to copy. That's not practical in a lot of cases. We might want to copy a folder and all of its files.

Recursive File Copying

Let's modify the configuration section of Gruntfile.js so it specifies folders as well as files:

files/recursive/deploying/Gruntfile.js
```
grunt.config.init({
  copyFiles: {
    options: {
      workingDirectory: 'working',
      manifest: [
        'index.html', 'stylesheets/', 'javascripts/'
      ]
    }
  }
});
```

If we tried to run our tasks right now we'd get errors because Grunt's built-in copy doesn't support directories. But we can iterate over the files and folders in our list and then detect if the entry is a file or a folder. If it's a file we can copy it like before, but if it's a folder we'll just have to iterate over the files and folders inside that folder. If you've done anything like this in other languages, you'll know that the solution is to use recursion. And Grunt provides a built-in function for that.

Currently, our copyFiles task loops over the files like this:

```
files/simple/deploying/Gruntfile.js
files.forEach(function(file) {
  var destination = workingDirectory + '/' + file;
  grunt.log.writeln('Copying ' + file + ' to ' + destination);
  grunt.file.copy(file, destination);
});
```

But let's change this task so it instead calls a function we'll create, called recursiveCopy():

```
files/recursive/deploying/Gruntfile.js
files.forEach(function(item) {
  recursiveCopy(item, workingDirectory);
});
```

The recursiveCopy() function takes in the source, which is either a file or folder, and the destination folder. This function then checks to see if the source is a file or a folder. If it's a file, we'll copy it. But if it's a folder, we'll have to dig into the files in the folder and call the recursiveCopy() function again. And if there are folders within folders, we'll have to handle those the same way. But thanks to the power of recursion, we can declare the function like this:

```
files/recursive/deploying/Gruntfile.js
var recursiveCopy = function(source, destination){
  if(grunt.file.isDir(source)){

    grunt.file.recurse(source, function(file){
      recursiveCopy(file, destination);
    });

  }else{
    grunt.log.writeln('Copying ' + source + ' to ' + destination);
    grunt.file.copy(source, destination + '/' + source);
  }
}
```

We use grunt.file.isDir() to detect whether the source element is a file or a directory. If it's a file, we print the file to the screen and do the file copy like before.

When the file is a directory, we use grunt.file.recurse(), which runs the callback function of our choice against each file or folder in the structure. When grunt.file.recurse() executes the callback, it sends the source file's absolute path as the first parameter. It can send the root directory, the current file's directory, and the current file's name as arguments if the callback function accepts them. But in our case we'll keep things really simple; we just pass the source to our recursiveCopy() function inside the callback.

A quick run of our copyFiles task shows it's working:

```
$ grunt copyFiles

Running "copyFiles" task
Copying index.html to working
Copying stylesheets/layout.css to working
Copying stylesheets/style.css to working
Copying javascripts/app.js to working

Done, without errors.
```

By combining a little JavaScript code with Grunt's built-in utilities, we can now clone a directory structure with ease.

Using Values from Files

Occasionally we'll want to use some of the values from package.json in our projects, such as the project name, the project author, or the license information. Grunt provides a function called file.readJSON() that, as you might be able to guess from the name, reads JSON data from a file and parses it into a JavaScript object. Add this to the configuration section of the Gruntfile:

files/recursive/deploying/Gruntfile.js
```
grunt.config.init({
  pkg: grunt.file.readJSON('package.json'),
```

It's very common to see something like this in a Gruntfile. We can use these and other configuration values throughout the Gruntfile in a couple of ways. First, we can just access them as properties of the configuration, like grunt.config.get('pkg.name'). But we can also use Grunt's templating engine.

When we copy files to the source folder, let's add a version.txt file that includes the name of the app and the version.

At the bottom of the copyFiles() task, add this code:

files/recursive/deploying/Gruntfile.js
```
var content = '<%=pkg.name %> version <%= pkg.version %>';
content = grunt.template.process(content);
grunt.file.write(workingDirectory + '/version.txt', content);
```

The grunt.template.process() function injects our configuration variables into the template string, giving us a new string that we can write into a file.

These template strings work automatically inside the Grunt configuration section too, without the need for the explicit call to grunt.template.process.. That means you can use templating to easily access configuration variables. For example, if you

Accessing Configuration inside Tasks

Using grunt.config.get() to retrieve values from inside of tasks works fine, but Grunt provides a handy shortcut. Inside a task, we can access this.options() to access the options property of our task's configuration. This lets us to change the tasks' name without having to change how we get the task's associated parameters.

files/options/deploying/Gruntfile.js
```
files = this.options().manifest;
workingDirectory = this.options().workingDirectory;
```

Grunt also provides this.requiresConfig() as a shortcut for checking configuration. Unfortunately, unlike this.options(), the this.requiresConfig() method doesn't look up values relative to the task. But by using this.name() to fetch the task name, we can remove all of the hard-coded configuration in the task, like this:

files/options/deploying/Gruntfile.js
```
grunt.registerTask('copyFiles', function(){
  var files, workingDirectory;
➤ this.requiresConfig(this.name + '.options.manifest');
➤ this.requiresConfig(this.name + '.options.workingDirectory');
➤
➤ files = this.options().manifest;
➤ workingDirectory = this.options().workingDirectory;

  files.forEach(function(item) {
    recursiveCopy(item, workingDirectory);
  });
```

This is a nice refactoring of the copyFiles task. But we can't do this for the clean and createFolder tasks since those use the copyFiles task's configuration values. We'll have to leave those alone.

wanted to use the value of the copyFiles.options.manifest variable in another task's configuration, you could reference it as <%= copyFiles.options.manifest %> instead.

Now, if we run grunt copyFiles again, in our working folder we'll get a new file called version.txt that contains this:

```
deploying version 0.0.0
```

This technique is great for injecting the name of the project, the authors, or even the licensing information into the headings of files.

What's Next?

Grunt's built-in file utilities make it easy to work with files and folders across operating systems. They form the foundation of many of Grunt's plug-ins. In addition, the templating mechanism can ease configuration and text generation. Before you move on, try these additional things:

- Inside the copyFiles task, use this.requires() to make the copyFiles task depend on the clean task.

- Break the code that creates the version.txt into its own task. Make sure it depends on the successful completion of the copyFiles task and add your new task to the deploy task.

Now let's look at multitasks, a powerful Grunt feature that many plug-ins rely on heavily.

CHAPTER 3

One Task, Many Outputs

So far we've looked at simple tasks, but sometimes it's handy to be able to define a single task that does many things at once. For example, let's say you were creating next week's new JavaScript framework and you wanted to create a full version and a micro version that includes only the basics. Using Grunt's *multitasks*, you can create a single task definition that iterates over a collection of targets and executes code against those targets with ease.

So what's a target? You could think of a target as a configuration group for a task. You set up a configuration block that specifies the target and the associated data:

```
concat: {
  basic: {
    src: ['src/awsome.js'],
    dest: 'dist/awesome.js',
  },
  full: {
    src: ['src/awesome.js', 'src/plugins/editor', 'src/plugins/hl.js'],
    dest: 'dist/awesome-full.js',
  },
},
```

The task then executes its code against all the targets you specify, using the data to determine what the task should do. Many Grunt plug-ins are implemented as multitasks.

In this chapter, we'll explore how multitasks work by working first with targets and data, and then with files.

Introducing Multitasks

Multitasks work by combining a task definition and a block of configuration that defines the targets. Unlike regular tasks, Grunt's multitasks automatically look for a configuration section that matches the name of the task. So let's create a simple configuration that explores how multitasks work.

We'll use Node.js and the Open Weather API to grab the current temperature of some zip codes. We'll configure the zip codes as targets and we'll write a task to fetch the data for the temperatures.

First, create a new folder and a package.json file:

```
$ mkdir weather
$ cd weather
$ npm init
```

When prompted for values, use the defaults for everything.

Next, install Grunt as a dependency:

```
$ npm install grunt --save-dev
```

Then create a new Gruntfile like you've done in previous chapters:

multitasks/weather/Gruntfile.js
```
module.exports = function(grunt){
}
```

Now, our plan is to use a multitask and some zip codes as targets. To do this, we define the configuration section using grunt.initConfig(), and then we specify the targets and some associated zip code for each target:

multitasks/weather/Gruntfile.js
```
grunt.config.init({
  weather: {
    home: 60623,
    work: 60622
  }
});
```

Now we can declare our task:

multitasks/weather/Gruntfile.js
```
grunt.registerMultiTask('weather', 'Fetches weather', function() {
});
```

The task's name has to match the configuration section for multitasks. When we run the task, it will automatically look for that configuration block.

Now we need to set up some variables. Inside a Grunt multitask we can access the target with this.target and we can access the data associated with that target with this.data.

multitasks/weather/Gruntfile.js
```
var done, http, location, request, requestOptions,  zipCode;

location = this.target;
zipCode = this.data;
```

The location name is the target, and the zip code is the data.

To make the actual request, we'll use Node's built-in http module. This module provides a request() method that takes an options object containing information about the type of request, the host, the port, and the path. We configure that like this:

multitasks/weather/Gruntfile.js
```
requestOptions = {
  host: 'api.openweathermap.org',
  path: '/data/2.5/weather?units=imperial&q=' + zipCode,
  port: 80,
  method: 'GET'
}
```

All that's left to do is make the request and parse the results. When we make the request, we'll get the data back in chunks, which we'll concatenate together. Then when we've gotten all the chunks, we'll join them together, parse the response as JSON data, and display the temperature.

multitasks/weather/Gruntfile.js
```
Line 1  http = require('http');

        done = this.async();

     5  request = http.request(requestOptions, function(response) {
          var buffer = [];

          response.on('data', function(data){
            buffer.push(data);
     10   });

          response.on('end', function(){
            var weather = JSON.parse(buffer.join());
            console.log(location + ' : ' + weather.main.temp + ' degrees');
     15

            done();

          });
        });
     20
        request.end();
```

Take a look at line 3. This line is incredibly important. Node's http module is asynchronous, so when we make a request for the weather data, Node doesn't wait for the response. Instead, it invokes the callback once the data gets back. Grunt, however, doesn't wait around. It'll finish the task run before we get our response.

Grunt has a workaround for this, though. We use this.async() to tell Grunt that this task is asynchronous, and that it should wait until we tell it we're done. So, on line 3 we create a variable called done by calling this.async(). Then on line 16, once we've parsed the response, we invoke done as a function, which tells Grunt we're all done. It's kind of a strange pattern, but it works really well.

When we run this task, we get our weather report. This book was written in the middle of a very cold winter, so what you're seeing are real Fahrenheit temperatures for the Chicago area:

```
$ grunt weather
Running "weather:home" (weather) task
home : 1.72 degrees

Running "weather:work" (weather) task
work : 1.85 degrees

Done, without errors.
```

If we added a new target and zip code, we'd get a third response. Multitasks make it very easy to configure a single task to handle multiple outputs.

Now let's look at something a little more practical: file concatenation.

Multitasks and Files

One of the most common uses for multitasks is in creating distribution packages for JavaScript libraries. To demonstrate, let's take the AngularJS library and create our own custom versions. We'll create one version that includes just AngularJS and the angular-resource library, and then a second version that also includes the jQuery library.

First, create a new folder called angular and then create a new package.json file in that folder using npm init:

```
$ mkdir angular
$ cd angular
$ npm init
```

For the settings, use the defaults. Or you could create your own package.json file that looks like this:

```
{
  "name": "AngularCustom",
  "version": "0.0.1",
  "description": "",
  "devDependencies": {
    "grunt": "~0.4.4"
  }
}
```

Then install Grunt as a project dependency with npm like we've done previously:

```
$ npm install grunt --save-dev
```

Then we need to create the Gruntfile itself, using the same skeleton we've used before:

multitasks/angular/Gruntfile.js
```
module.exports = function(grunt){
}
```

Next we need AngularJS and jQuery. We could download those from the Web, but there's a quicker way.

Fetching Client-Side Libraries with Bower

Bower is a package manager for client-side libraries, and it's a great way to quickly grab the libraries our project needs. Bower downloads any libraries we specify into a bower_components folder in our project. First, we'll install Bower globally:

```
$ npm install -g bower
```

Bower uses the Git version-control system to fetch libraries, so you'll need to install the Git command-line client on your computer. You can get installers for your operating system at the Git website.[1] And if you're on Windows, you'll need to install Git so that it runs from your Windows Command Prompt, not the default "Bash shell" option. See the Bower website for instructions on this.[2]

In addition, if you just installed Git, you may need to close and reopen your Terminal window before you can use it.

But once Bower's all set up, we can use it to fetch Angular and the other libraries, like this:

---

1. http://git-scm.com/downloads
2. http://bower.io/

```
$ bower install angular
$ bower install angular-resource
$ bower install jquery
```

Now, if you look under the bower_components folder, you'll see folders for angular, angular-resource, and jquery, with the appropriate JavaScript libraries in each folder. That's a lot easier than finding, downloading, unzipping, and moving a bunch of files around, isn't it?

Because we didn't specify any version info, Bower just grabs the latest version it knows about, and that's good enough for this demonstration.

One last thing before we move on; Bower is great about fetching remote libraries, but the authors of these libraries don't always use the same folder structure or naming scheme. For example, jQuery puts the library we need in a dist folder, while other libraries might place the files in a lib folder. Other libraries might require us to do some manual steps to produce a library we can include in our web application. So, when you use Bower inspect the files it downloads carefully to find what you're looking for.

Configuring Targets

We're going to have one task with two targets. Our first target will include only AngularJS and the angular-resource library. Our other target, which we'll call angularWithJquery, will also include jQuery. The following diagram illustrates exactly how this will work.

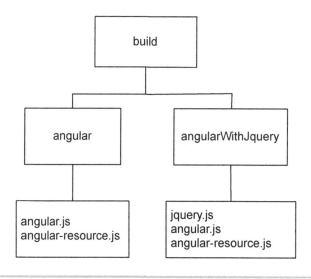

Figure 1—Our build task and its targets

When we run the build task, the individual targets will be created using the source files we specify.

So, using grunt.initConfig(), let's create the configuration for our build task. We specify the targets and their respective sources and destinations:

multitasks/angular/Gruntfile.js
```
grunt.config.init({
  build: {
    angular: {
      src: ['bower_components/angular/angular.js',
            'bower_components/angular-resource/angular-resource.js'],
      dest: 'dist/angular.js'
    },
    angularWithjQuery: {
      src: ['bower_components/jquery/dist/jquery.js',
            'bower_components/angular/angular.js',
            'bower_components/angular-resource/angular-resource.js'],
      dest: 'dist/jquery-angular.js'
    }
  }
});
```

We're specifying the source as an array of files, and the destination as a string. To write the task, we'll just have to iterate over the source files, join them together, and write out the destination file. Many common Grunt plug-ins use this approach, as Grunt favors configuration over coding.

But since we're writing our own multitask, we'll have to do some coding. Let's see how Grunt makes it easy for us to work with multiple targets and files.

Writing the Task

You've already seen how a multitask works. We can access the targets as an array. We iterate over the targets and grab the sources, read the contents of each file, and create a new file using the destination. The whole thing looks like this:

multitasks/angular/Gruntfile.js
```
Line 1  grunt.registerMultiTask('build', 'Concatenate files.', function() {
     2    var output = '';
     3    this.files.forEach(function(filegroup) {
     4      sources = filegroup.src.map(function(file){
     5        return(grunt.file.read(file));
     6      });
     7      output = sources.join(';');
     8      grunt.file.write(filegroup.dest, output);
     9    });
    10  });
```

On line 3 we iterate over the various targets. In a multitask, we use the files property to access the configured targets and their associated source and destination paths. This is cool because we don't have to worry about how the task was configured, as Grunt allows for several methods of configuring targets and destinations. All we have to do is iterate over the files array in our task.

On line 4 we use JavaScript's map() function on the source files, using the src property. This is a quick way to iterate over all of the source files, read their contents, and store them in a new array, and is a lot more appropriate than using a standard for loop and concatenating strings.

Since we've stored all the file contents in an array, we can join them together using join() and then write the output file to disk.

This code is very similar to the code used by the more "official" grunt-contrib-concat plug-in, but our version doesn't handle missing source files gracefully. So why did we build our own? Because now you have a good understanding of how Grunt can work with groups of files. When the next new JavaScript or CSS preprocessor comes out, you'll be able to write your own tasks to process your files. However, you can use Grunt's grunt.file.exists() to check for a file before reading it in.

At this point, we can run

```
$ grunt build
```

and we'll have a new dist folder with the two versions of our library. Best of all, we can run the targets independently by specifying them directly with grunt build:angular or grunt build:angularWithJquery.

What's Next?

Multitasks are incredibly important in Grunt. Many plug-ins are built around multitasks and they rely on a configuration similar to what we've used in this chapter. The concept of targets in Grunt is similar to how it works in Make and other build tools, and so you can use this approach for more than just concatenation of files. Before moving on, spend some time exploring the following:

- Modify the concatenation task we built so that it checks for the existence of source files and stops the task. You can use the filter() method on the filegroup.src array to silently remove missing files or display a warning message, but instead see if you can stop this and any subsequent tasks from firing.

- Right now, when our task concatenates files, it places a semicolon character between files. By using a configuration variable, allow users to specify the character used here.

Now that you understand more about multitasks and configuration, let's put several existing Grunt plug-ins together and configure them to make a modern web application's development process pain-free.

CHAPTER 4

Build a Workflow

Modern web apps, especially ones with plentiful client-side code, have a lot of resources and dependencies. Grunt makes wrangling those much easier.

In this chapter we'll create a simple Markdown editor with a live preview. The end result will look like the following figure.

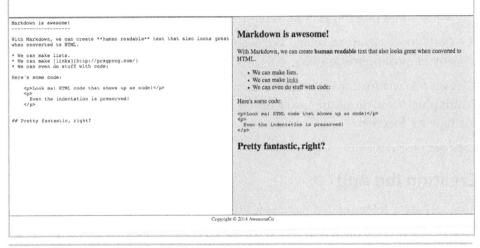

Figure 2—Our Markdown editor

We'll lean heavily on several technologies to make this work. We'll use the Angular web framework to build the app, and we'll use markdown.js to do the actual Markdown conversion. To make things more interesting, we'll use Sass, a CSS preprocessor, and we'll use CoffeeScript instead of JavaScript.

The focus of this exercise is to show how to use Grunt as a build tool for an application, and by using Angular, CoffeeScript, and Sass, we can explore how easy Grunt makes it to compile, combine, and minify assets while we work on the application. Even if you've never used Angular, Sass, or Coffee-Script before, you should have no problem following along.

To pull this off we'll build up a Gruntfile that does the following:

1. Converts all of the CoffeeScript files into JavaScript and puts the resulting JavaScript in a temporary folder

2. Concatenates Angular and the Markdown library we're using with the application logic we just converted from CoffeeScript to make a single app.js file

3. Minifies that app.js file, storing it in assets/app.js, which is where our web page will look for it

4. Adds support for Sass, the CSS preprocessor, by adding a file watcher and then doing a compilation similar to what we did with CoffeeScript

5. Sets things up so that any time we change a CoffeeScript or Sass file, the whole build process gets kicked off

6. Configures Grunt to reload our web browser when we make changes to any of our application files

We won't be writing these Grunt tasks ourselves. Instead we'll rely on several Grunt plug-ins to do all the heavy lifting. We'll just need to configure the plug-ins to work together.

Let's get started!

Creating the App

First, create a folder called markdown, and inside of that folder create folders for the CoffeeScript files, the Sass files, and the assets folder, which is where our finalized JavaScript and CSS files will go.

```
$ mkdir markdown
$ cd markdown
$ mkdir coffeescript
$ mkdir sass
$ mkdir assets
```

Next, we'll need the Angular framework, the Markdown.js library for converting Markdown code to HTML, and the angular-sanitize library so we can push raw HTML back into the interface.[1,2,3] Without the sanitation library, Angular won't let us use the output from the Markdown converter.

To get those libraries, we'll use Bower like we did in *Fetching Client-Side Libraries with Bower*, on page 25. Run the following commands:

```
$ bower install angular
$ bower install angular-sanitize
$ bower install markdown#0.6.0-beta1
```

We need to build the client-side version of the Markdown library so we can use it in our web application, and we can do that easily thanks to a Grunt task distributed with the library. Execute the following commands:

```
$ cd bower_components/markdown
$ npm install
$ cd ../../
```

Running the npm install command inside of the project installs the projects' dependencies and then runs a Grunt task that builds the distributions for the project. The JavaScript file we need is now located in the bower_components/markdown/dist folder.

If you're unable to download the libraries using Bower, you can find everything you need in the workflows folder of the book's downloadable source code, along with this completed project.

Now let's look at the application code itself.

The App Logic

Here's how the user interface works: There's a single <textarea> field on the page, and we're using Angular to watch that field for changes. When data in that field changes, the updatePreview() method gets called. This method will use a simple service in Angular to convert the input to HTML. The results get placed back on the page in the update area.

All of the application's logic will be stored in several separate CoffeeScript files, which will make it easy for us to find things later on. We're using Coffee-Script for our application logic, and *CoffeeScript: Accelerated JavaScript Development [Bur11]* does a great job of covering how CoffeeScript works. However, the code we're using should be easy enough to understand.

---

1.   http://code.angularjs.org/1.2.10/angular.js
2.   https://github.com/evilstreak/markdown-js/releases
3.   http://code.angularjs.org/1.2.10/angular-sanitize.js

Our Angular app uses a basic module called MarkdownEditor, and we define that in coffeescript/app.coffee like this:

workflow/markdown/coffeescript/app.coffee
```
@MarkdownEditor = angular.module("markdownEditor", [])
```

Next, we define the controller that is bound to the HTML page. This controller is what makes it possible to get the data from the page and push the results back to the page:

workflow/markdown/coffeescript/controllers/main_controller.coffee
```
# The controller
@MarkdownEditor.controller "MainCtrl", ['$scope','$sce', 'MarkdownConverter',
($scope, $sce, MarkdownConverter) ->
  $scope.updatePreview = ->
    converted = MarkdownConverter.convert($scope.input)
    $scope.output = $sce.trustAsHtml(converted)
]
```

This controller uses a service called MarkdownConverter, which we define in coffee-script/factories/markdown_converter.coffee:

workflow/markdown/coffeescript/factories/markdown_converter.coffee
```
@MarkdownEditor.factory "MarkdownConverter", ->

  convert: (input) ->
    markdown.toHTML input
```

This service uses the markdown.js library to do the conversion. Although this code is fairly trivial, the markdown.js library can do additional transformations, and if we wanted to do those transformations, encapsulating them in this factory would keep our code clean and separated.

That takes care of the program logic. Thanks to Angular, there wasn't much to do.

Creating the Interface

The logic is in place, so now we can connect it to our interface, which is just a simple HTML page with a text area and an output region. Create the file index.html with the following code:

workflow/markdown/index.html
```
<!DOCTYPE html>
<html lang="en-US">
  <head>
    <meta charset="utf-8">
    <title>Markdown Editor</title>
    <link rel="stylesheet" href="assets/app.css">
  </head>
```

```
     <body ng-app="markdownEditor">
       <header class="masthead">
10       <h1>MarkDownMark Editor</h1>
       </header>

       <div class="content" ng-controller="MainCtrl">
         <section class="editor">
15         <textarea class="input"
                     ng-model="input"
                     ng-change="updatePreview()">
           </textarea>
         </section>
20
         <section id="output" class="preview" ng-bind-html="output"></section>

       </div>

25     <footer>
         <small>Copyright &copy; 2014 AwesomeCo</small>
       </footer>

       <script src="assets/app.js"></script>
30
     </body>
   </html>
```

Notice the <body> tag. The ng-app attribute is an Angular directive that specifies the module we're using. Then on line 13 we wire up the controller we want to use with the ng-controller attribute. Everything inside of this element is scoped to the controller. So the controller's methods are visible to the view, and the fields we bind using ng-model or ng-click are visible to the controller.

This page loads a single app.js file at the bottom. To keep our app easy to develop, we've kept its components in separate files. We'll use Grunt to merge them all together next.

Wrangling the JavaScript

Our index.html file is looking for a file called assets/app.js, but all we have are several separate CoffeeScript files. Using Grunt, we'll compile those CoffeeScript files into a single JavaScript file, then combine that file with the Angular and Markdown libraries, creating a single file we can bring into our document. And to ensure that the file downloads even faster, we'll minify it, which will remove whitespace and rename variables and functions to reduce the overall file size considerably.

Compiling CoffeeScript

Let's set up a basic package.json and Gruntfile for our app. First, create package.json with the following contents:

```
{
  "name": "MarkdownEditor",
  "version": "0.0.1",
  "description": "A simple markdown editing app",
  "main": "index.html",
  "author": "Max Power",
}
```

Next, create the Gruntfile.js file in the root of the application with the usual skeleton:

workflow/markdown/Gruntfile.js
```
module.exports = function(grunt){
};
```

With those in place, we can install grunt and the grunt-contrib-coffee plug-in with npm:

```
$ npm install grunt --save-dev
$ npm install grunt-contrib-coffee --save-dev
```

And now we can configure the CoffeeScript plug-in to build the JavaScript files our browsers crave.

Chunked Configuration

So far we've used Grunt's initConfig() function to set up configuration variables. But we're going to create a somewhat complex Gruntfile that might be hard to follow after awhile. Grunt offers a more modular way for us to define configurations with its config() function. This lets us define our configuration in manageable pieces. Add this to the Gruntfile:

workflow/markdown/Gruntfile.js
```
grunt.loadNpmTasks('grunt-contrib-coffee');
grunt.config('coffee', {
  app: {
    options: {
      bare: false
    },
    files: {
      'tmp/compiled.js': ['coffeescript/app.coffee',
                          'coffeescript/factories/*.coffee',
                          'coffeescript/controllers/*.coffee']
    }
  }
});
```

As you might be able to guess, the loadNpmModule() loads a Grunt plug-in. Once we load the plug-in, we can configure it.

The CoffeeScript plug-in is designed as a multitask, so we'll have to specify targets even though we'll have only a single one. We'll call our target app and then specify the files. The files key uses a simple JavaScript object, where we specify the destination file as the key, and then an array of source files as the value.

In some cases, you might be able to get away with just specifying coffeescript/ **/*.coffee as the source, which would take all of the CoffeeScript files found within the coffeescript folder. But by being a little more specific, we can ensure that things are included in the right order.

In the Terminal, run the command grunt coffee, and you'll see the output:

```
$ grunt coffee
Running "coffee:app" (coffee) task

Done, without errors.
```

Now, provided that we didn't make any typos in our CoffeeScript files, we'll see a new folder, called tmp in our project. It contains a new file called compiled.js that holds the compiled version of our CoffeeScript files. The separate files were stitched together into compiled.js. We're not done with this file, though.

Concatenating JavaScript

The CoffeeScript compilation task put all of our application files into a single file when it converted them. But we're going to bundle up the Angular libraries along with our own code to create a single JavaScript file.

We wrote our own simple task to do concatenation back in Chapter 3, *One Task, Many Outputs*, on page 21, but this time we'll use the grunt-contrib-concat plug-in instead, as it's more flexible than what we wrote. To install it use npm as follows:

```
$ npm install grunt-contrib-concat --save-dev
```

Once the plug-in is installed, we require it in our configuration file and configure it the same way we did with the CoffeeScript plug-in.

```
workflow/markdown/Gruntfile.js
grunt.loadNpmTasks('grunt-contrib-concat');
grunt.config('concat', {
  scripts: {
    src: ['bower_components/angular/angular.js',
          'bower_components/angular-sanitize/angular-sanitize.js',
```

```
        'bower_components/markdown/dist/markdown.js',
        'tmp/compiled.js'],
  dest: 'tmp/app.js'
  }
});
```

We pull in the required libraries from the components folders, along with the file generated by our CoffeeScript code. We place the output back in the tmp folder because we're not quite done with it yet.

Let's run the task:

```
$ grunt concat
Running "concat:scripts" (concat) task
File "tmp/app.js" created.

Done, without errors.
```

We're almost finished with the JavaScript side of things. However, the JavaScript file we just created is quite large. Let's shrink it down.

Minifying JavaScript

To make our JavaScript download faster, we're going to minify it. This process removes comments, whitespace, and line breaks, and even obfuscates code by shortening variable names. We'll use the Uglify utility to do this by way of the grunt-contrib-uglify plug-in.

First, we install the plug-in:

```
$ npm install grunt-contrib-uglify --save-dev
```

By now you can probably guess how we'll configure this. One of the nice things about Grunt plug-ins is they share a level of consistency. In the Gruntfile, load the plug-in and then add the configuration section, placing the output in the assets folder, which is where our index.html file looks for the JavaScript file.

```
workflow/markdown/Gruntfile.js
grunt.loadNpmTasks('grunt-contrib-uglify');
grunt.config('uglify', {
  scripts: {
    files: {
      'assets/app.js' : 'tmp/app.js'
    }
  }
});
```

And that takes care of the JavaScript! Test it out by running the following:

```
$ grunt uglify
Running "uglify:scripts" (uglify) task
File assets/app.js created: 816.58 kB → 128.81 kB

Done, without errors.
```

The task's output shows us that by uglifying the content, we've turned more than 800 KB of JavaScript code into only 128 KB. That's going to make the application download a lot faster, and illustrates why this minification process has become part of a modern workflow.

And that's it for the JavaScript code.

Adding Some Style

Our application would look a lot better with some styling. Writing pure CSS is incredibly limiting, though. Using a CSS preprocessor improves things greatly. With a preprocessor, you can produce CSS using variables, loops, functions, and intelligent selector inheritance. Like CoffeeScript, you run Sass files through a processor that generates regular, well-formatted CSS files for use in the browser. There are a lot of preprocessors out there, but Sass is one of the most advanced.[4] Covering Sass in detail is out of scope for this book, but if you want to know more, look at *Pragmatic Guide to Sass [CC11]*. For this exercise, we'll just place some prewritten code in the project so we can set up our Grunt tasks.

To use Sass, you need to have the Ruby programming language installed. On OS X, you already have what you need. On Windows you can download an installer for Ruby called RubyInstaller.[5] Install that using the defaults, and you're ready to go. On Linux you can install Ruby using your package manager.

With Ruby installed, you can execute this command:

```
$ gem install sass
```

The gem command is like npm but for Ruby libraries.

Creating Styles with Sass

Using Sass, we can easily break up our styles into separate files, making things easy to organize. And, like CoffeeScript, Sass can stitch these files together automatically if we structure them properly.

---

4.   http://sass-lang.org
5.   http://rubyinstaller.org/

Let's define the site's layout so it looks like the interface in Figure 2, *Our Markdown editor*, on page 31, with a header, a footer, and a middle region split into two panes. Our editor will be on the left and the live preview will be on the right.

To pull this off we'll use some absolute positioning. Using Sass, we can define *mixins*, reusable named chunks of code we can "mix in" to our CSS rules. In the file sass/_layout.scss add the following code:

workflow/markdown/sass/_layout.scss
```
@mixin row{
  box-sizing: border-box;
  overflow: hidden;
  position: absolute;
  left: 0;
  right: 0;
}

@mixin col{
  overflow: hidden;
  position: absolute;
  top: 0;
  bottom: 0;
}
```

In this file we're defining two mixins; one for rows and one for columns. We'll use them in our main stylesheet next. The filename starts with an underscore because it's a "partial" file, which is meant to be pulled into another Sass file. Grunt's Sass task will skip any file with an underscore when it converts our files.

To use this partial, we create the file sass/style.scss and add this to the top:

workflow/markdown/sass/style.scss
```
@import 'layout';
```

This merges the contents of _layout.scss into this file. We can now use those mixins we defined.

One of Sass's best features is the ability to use variables for things like colors. Let's define two variables for colors in this stylesheet:

```
$backgroundColor: #DDD;
$borderColor: #000;
```

Variables in Sass start with a dollar sign, and we use a colon instead of the equals sign to assign the value to the variable.

Beneath the variables, add the code to define the header, footer, and middle section of the interface. We want the header and footer to be 100% wide, and we want the editor and the preview pane to sit side by side. First, we divide the page into three horizontal rows that stretch the full width of the page:

```
Line 1  body{ margin: 0; }

     -  header{
     -    @include row;
     5    height: 100px;
     -  }

     -  .content{
     -    @include row;
    10    overflow-y: auto;
     -    top: 100px;
     -    bottom: 50px;
     -  }

    15  footer{
     -    @include row;
     -    bottom: 0;
     -    height: 50px;
     -    text-align: center;
    20  }
```

On line 4 we make a call to our row mixin, which brings the properties of that mixin into the CSS rule. This way we don't have to repeat style rules manually, and we also don't have to add classes like row or col to our HTML code.

Next we align the preview pane and the editor pane:

```
Line 1  .editor, .preview{
     -    @include col;
     -    width: 50%;
     -    background-color: $backgroundColor;
     5    border: 1px solid $borderColor;
     -  }

     -  textarea.input{
     -    height: 100%;
    10    padding: 1%;
     -    width: 100%;
     -  }

     -  .preview{
    15    padding: 1%;
     -    right: 0;
     -  }
```

On line 2 we apply the col mixin to the editor and the preview pane and set the width for both to 50%. Then, on line 4 and the line that follows, we use the Sass variables for the values of our colors instead of hard-coding the values like we would with normal CSS. Finally, we style the text box and the preview pane.

This takes care of the code for the interface, but our interface won't look any different yet because we've written this code with a CSS preprocessor. Let's get Grunt to turn this Sass into CSS so our browser can actually use it.

Adding Sass to Grunt

By this point you can probably guess how this will work. There's a plug-in called grunt-contrib-sass that we have to install and configure. So, install the plug-in with npm:

```
$ npm install grunt-contrib-sass --save-dev
```

Then add the following configuration to the Gruntfile:

```
workflow/markdown/Gruntfile.js
grunt.loadNpmTasks('grunt-contrib-sass');
grunt.config('sass', {
  app: {
    files: {
      'tmp/app.css': ['sass/style.scss']
    }
  }
});
```

Notice that we only need to convert the sass/style.scss file. The partial file gets included in that file. However, if we specified the partial, or we used a wildcard pattern like sass/*.scss, the Sass plug-in is smart enough to ignore any files with underscores.

Notice that we placed the output file in the tmp folder. We're not quite done with the stylesheet yet.

Minifying Our CSS

We've minified the JavaScript code in our app, and now we'll do the same with our CSS. We'll use the grunt-contrib-cssmin plug-in to do this, and the configuration for this is very easy. First, install the plug-in as a dependency:

```
$ npm install grunt-contrib-cssmin --save-dev
```

Then, configure it almost exactly like the uglify task for JavaScript, by reading in the tmp/app.css file that the Sass task created and placing the minified version in the assets/ folder:

```
workflow/markdown/Gruntfile.js
grunt.loadNpmTasks('grunt-contrib-cssmin');
grunt.config('cssmin', {
  app: {
    files: {
      'assets/app.css': ['tmp/app.css']
    }
  }
});
```

Now let's run the cssmin task to generate the assets/app.css file that our interface wants:

```
$ grunt sass cssmin
Running "cssmin:app" (cssmin) task
File assets/app.css created: 1 kB → 537 B
Done, without errors.
```

The task runs perfectly, cutting our file size nearly in half. And now we have all the components of our workflow, as well as a completely working application that you should be able to view by opening index.html in your browser.

But wow, what a lot of steps. Let's simplify this whole process with a build task that runs all of the steps.

Simplifying the Build

In Chapter 1, *The Very Basics*, on page 1, you learned how to make a task that calls other tasks. Let's do the same thing here. We want one task that, when called, invokes the tasks to build the JavaScript files and the CSS files. Let's add a build task to our Gruntfile:

```
workflow/markdown/Gruntfile.js
grunt.registerTask('build', "Builds the application.",
                   ['coffee', 'concat:scripts', 'sass', 'cssmin', 'uglify' ]);
```

When we execute this build task, the whole process runs.

```
$ grunt build
Running "coffee:app" (coffee) task

Running "concat:scripts" (concat) task
File "tmp/app.js" created.

Running "sass:app" (sass) task
File tmp/app.css created.
```

```
Running "cssmin:app" (cssmin) task
File assets/app.css created.

Running "uglify:scripts" (uglify) task
File assets/app.js created.

Done, without errors.
```

And that is ridiculously cool. A single command builds our application, letting us take advantage of powerful preprocessors and minification tools. But we can do better than this.

Watching Files for Changes

We've set up a ton of tasks so far, but every time we make a change to a file we have to run Grunt manually. And we really should never have to do anything manually when it comes to task management. Let's use the grunt-contrib-watch plug-in to watch files for changes and run the appropriate tasks.

Install the plug-in first:

```
$ npm install grunt-contrib-watch --save-dev
```

To configure this plug-in, we specify a target, the files to watch, and the Grunt tasks that should run when those files change. For our JavaScript files, we'll actually want to watch the CoffeeScript files for changes. When those files change, we'll need to run the coffee(), concat(), and uglify() tasks. Then we'll want to watch the CSS files for changes and run the sass and cssmin tasks. So first, let's set up the configuration to watch the JavaScript files:

```
workflow/markdown/Gruntfile.js
grunt.loadNpmTasks('grunt-contrib-watch');

grunt.config('watch', {
  scripts: {
    files: ['coffeescripts/**/*.coffee'],
    tasks: ['coffee', 'concat:scripts', 'uglify'],

    options: {
      spawn: false
    }
  },
});
```

And then, inside of that configuration block, we'll add another target for the Sass files:

workflow/markdown/Gruntfile.js

```
styles: {
  files: ['sass/**/*.scss'],
  tasks: ['sass', 'cssmin'],
  options: {
    spawn: false
  }
},
```

To use this, we employ the grunt watch command. Unlike other tasks, Grunt doesn't return to the command line. Instead, it stays running in a loop, watching files for changes. Open one of the Sass files or the CoffeeScript files, make a change, save the file, and watch the changes happen.

To stop watching, press Ctrl-C.

Refreshing the Browser Automatically

The grunt-contrib-watch plug-in has built-in support for LiveReload, an amazing tool that can automatically reload web pages and CSS documents in the browser whenever files change. This is incredibly useful for any web developer, so let's configure it.

All we have to do is add a few additional options to the configuration section for the grunt-contrib-watch plug-in. First, we'll configure it to watch for changes to the index.html file. We won't need to run any tasks when that file changes. And then we'll include the option to enable LiveReload support.

workflow/markdown/Gruntfile.js

```
interface: {
  files: ['index.html']
},
options: {
  livereload: true
}
```

To see this in action, you'll need to download the extension for your web browser. You can get extensions for Chrome, Firefox, and Safari from the LiveReload website.[6] Install the plug-in, then fire up grunt-watch in your Terminal and activate the plug-in. Then change something in the HTML or the CSS and see the page update after you save the file.

LiveReload is one of the most powerful tools a modern web developer has. Being able to see the changes live without having to refresh the page manually dramatically speeds up the development process, especially when you're

---

6. http://feedback.livereload.com/knowledgebase/articles/86242-how-do-i-install-and-use-the-browser-extensions-

modifying a site's design. Since Grunt makes this so easy to set up, you should make it part of your workflow immediately.

What's Next?

That was quite a trek, but as a result we have a simple, structured, and easy-to-follow configuration file for our application's build process. We can use this as we develop new features for our app, and even to prepare the application for production. Your applications don't have to use CoffeeScript or Sass (although I strongly suggest using a CSS preprocessor instead of writing CSS by hand), but grunt-contrib-concat and grunt-contrib-watch will hopefully find their way into your next project's workflow. But don't move on to the next chapter just yet; try these first:

- Investigate other plug-ins for your workflow, such as grunt-contrib-jshint, which checks your JavaScript files for errors, or grunt-contrib-imagemin, which can automatically compress images.[7,8]

- Use the preprocess option for scripts in the package.json file to call the grunt build task whenever you run npm install. This will make it easy for someone who works on your app to get started with it.

- Investigate Yeoman,[9] a tool that incorporates project creation with Grunt and gives you a workflow like this automatically, with generators for specific projects.

We've integrated a ton of cool plug-ins, but now let's look into what makes up a Grunt plug-in as we create our own. Go on—turn the page!

CHAPTER 5

Create a Plug-in

As you've already seen, plug-ins let you share functionality across projects or with other people, easily extending Grunt's features. In this chapter we'll create a simple Grunt plug-in that lets us quickly open in a web browser the page we're working on. This may seem superfluous, but it lets us explore the process of creating a plug-in, and it allows us to call out to an external program. Plus, when you're done you'll have a plug-in you can invoke as part of a larger process. For example, at the end of a build you can make your application's start page open in the browser so you can see if things are working well.

The Structure of a Plug-in

A basic Grunt plug-in consists of a tasks folder that contains one or more JavaScript files that define the tasks. These files have the exact same structure as a regular Gruntfile.

Inside of the tasks folder is a lib folder that should hold any functions or objects that do the work. In other words, your task definitions go in the main tasks folder and the logic for those tasks goes in the lib folder. If you explore the official Grunt plug-ins you'll see that this is the structure they use. It keeps the task definitions clean and concise.

The plug-in also has a package.json folder and a Gruntfile.js file. The Gruntfile.js file has a line that loads the tasks from the tasks folder, which makes it easy to try out your plug-in.

Now that you know how plug-ins are structured, let's build our plug-in's core functionality.

Creating the Plug-in Skeleton

First, create a new folder called grunt-open-with-chrome. Navigate into that folder and create another folder called tasks. Then run the npm init command to create the package.json file for the plug-in in that new folder:

```
$ mkdir grunt-open-with-chrome
$ cd grunt-open-with-chrome
$ mkdir tasks
$ npm init
```

When you run the generator, you'll have to answer the usual questions. For this exercise, answer them as follows:

1. Leave the project name as the default.

2. For the description, use "Open the page in Chrome."

3. Leave the version number as the default value.

4. For the project Git repository, leave it as a default or enter a valid Git URL if you'd like to push your code to a Git repository.

5. Leave the project home page, the issue tracker, and the license at their default values.

6. Enter your name for the author name.

7. Enter your email for the author email.

8. Leave all of the other values at their defaults.

Next, run the following to install Grunt, because we'll want to be able to test out our Grunt plug-ins:

```
$ npm install grunt --save-dev
```

Building Our Plug-in's Logic

Our plug-in's main goal is to let a user open a web page or a URL with Grunt. Ideally, we'd like it to work like this:

```
$ grunt open:index.html
```

And then it would open that page in Google Chrome. To do this, we'll have to detect the platform we're running on so we can find out how to launch Chrome, and we'll have to use some mechanism to make Grunt launch an external program. Grunt comes with grunt.util.spawn(), which is perfect for this.

Calling External Apps from Grunt

To call an external file from Grunt, we use Node.js's built-in child_process module.

The exec() method is a perfect fit for this situation. It takes in two arguments: the command we want to run and a callback function that executes when the command finishes. For example, if we wanted to run the ls -alh command, we'd do this:

```
var exec = require('child_process').exec;
process = exec('ls -alh', function (error, stdout, stderr) {
  // whatever we want to do after the program finishes.
});
```

In the callback, we can check for error messages from the external program and handle them accordingly.

To launch Google Chrome in a way that works on multiple operating systems, we'll have to dynamically create the command we pass to exec(), using different system commands and arguments for each operating system. So let's build an object that does that for us.

Creating a Module for Our Launcher

To keep the code for our tasks clean, we're going to encapsulate all of the logic we'll need to launch Google Chrome in its own Node.js module.

We'll start by creating a file called lib/chrome_launcher.js that contains the following code:

```
grunt-open-with-chrome/tasks/lib/chrome_launcher.js
module.exports.init = function(grunt){

  // the object we'll return
  var exports = {};
  // returns the object
  return(exports);
};
```

This is a common pattern in object-oriented JavaScript and in Node.js apps, called the Revealing Module Pattern. We use module.exports() to define what objects or functions this module exposes. With the Revealing Module Pattern we define a function that returns a JavaScript object that we create. This allows us to have both public and private methods on this object.

Our main JavaScript program will use this module by requiring it and calling the init() function, which then returns the object represented by our exports object. This init() function takes a reference to Grunt, and is a very common approach used by authors of Grunt plug-ins.

Inside of the init() function we add the function that creates the command based on the operating system the user is running. We use Node's process.platform() method to detect the operating system. If it's Windows it'll start with win, and if it's Linux it'll start with linux. If it's a Mac it'll be darwin, but we'll make that the default case. Here's how we do all of that:

grunt-open-with-chrome/tasks/lib/chrome_launcher.js
```
// creates the command
var createCommand = function(file){
  // booleans for the OS we're using
  var command = "";
  var linux = !!process.platform.match(/^linux/);
  var windows = !!process.platform.match(/^win/);
  if(windows){
    command = 'start chrome ' + file;
  }else if (linux){
    command = 'google-chrome "' + file + '"';
  }else{
    command = 'open -a "Google Chrome" ' + file;
  }
  return(command);
};
```

On Windows we use the start command to launch a program. On OS X we have to use the open command, and on Linux we call the program directly. Each of these programs accepts slightly different options, and we have to properly escape the paths to the program and the arguments for each operating system.

Finally, we need to define the public method, which we'll call open(). This method will use Node.js's exec() method to launch Google Chrome. It'll take the file we want to open as its first argument, and a second argument that references the done() function. In *Introducing Multitasks*, on page 21, we saw that Grunt doesn't wait for long-running tasks to finish. We have to tell Grunt to wait until we call the done() function. If we don't do this, we won't be able to see any error messages because Grunt will quit before the callback on exec() can finish.

So, with all that in mind, we define this open() method inside the init() function as well:

grunt-open-with-chrome/tasks/lib/chrome_launcher.js
```
// opens Chrome and loads the file or URL passed in
exports.open = function(file, done){
  var command, process, exec;
```

```
    command = createCommand(file);
    grunt.log.writeln('Running command: ' + command);

    exec = require('child_process').exec;
    process = exec(command, function (error, stdout, stderr) {
      if (error) {
        if(error.code !== 0){
          grunt.warn(stderr);
          grunt.log.writeln(error.stack);
        }
      }
      done();
    });
};
```

We use the createCommand() function to get the command we need for our OS, and then we execute the process with that command. Then in the callback we check to see to see if the process worked. If it returned an exit code of 0, everything went well. If it didn't, then the program didn't launch properly. But in either case, that's where we invoke the done() function to tell Grunt we're finished.

Notice that this method is attached to the module we're exporting. That will make it visible to the Grunt task. All of the other methods we defined are private ones.

That takes care of the basic implementation. All that's left is to make it available to Grunt.

The Grunt Task

Our Grunt task needs to take in the filename as its argument and then invoke the open() method we just created. Create the file tasks/open_with_chrome.js and add the following code:

grunt-open-with-chrome/tasks/open_with_chrome.js
```
'use strict';

module.exports = function(grunt) {
};
```

That should look strikingly similar to what you saw back in Chapter 1, *The Very Basics*, on page 1, when you created your first Gruntfile. Remember, a Grunt plug-in is just a Gruntfile stored in a special location.

Now we can require our custom module and define our task. We invoke our open() method, passing it the filename from the task along with the done function reference:

grunt-open-with-chrome/tasks/open_with_chrome.js
```
var chromeLauncher = require('./lib/chrome_launcher.js').init(grunt);
grunt.registerTask('open', 'Opens the file or URL with Chrome',
  function(file){
    var done = this.async();
    chromeLauncher.open(file, done);
  }
);
```

At this point we can test this out. To do that, we'll create a Gruntfile in the root of our project that contains the typical Grunt boilerplate and a line that loads all of the tasks in the tasks folder. So, create Gruntfile.js as the package.json file:

grunt-open-with-chrome/Gruntfile.js
```
'use strict';
module.exports = function(grunt) {
  grunt.loadTasks('tasks');
};
```

We can now run the plug-in by typing this:

```
$ grunt open:Gruntfile.js
```

Our Gruntfile pops open in the browser. We can specify any file we want, and we can even handle URLs, like this:

```
$ grunt open:http\://google.com
```

However, because Grunt uses the colon character as an argument separator, we have to escape the colon with a backslash character or it won't work.

When we run that command, Google Chrome pops up, displaying the URL we specified! Not a bad bit of work.

You can use this structure on your own Grunt projects too. Instead of putting all of the Grunt tasks in a single Gruntfile, we can modularize them under the tasks folder. Our main Gruntfile can hold all of the configuration and the tasks themselves can be nicely tucked away, out of sight and out of mind.

Using JSHint to Check for Errors and Problems

We've written quite a bit of JavaScript code in this chapter; some of it might not work right, and some of it might not conform to coding standards that other Grunt plug-ins want. We can use JSHint to detect errors and problems so we can fix them.[1] And best of all, we can do it easily with Grunt.

---

1. https://github.com/jshint/jshint

Specifying Compatibility with Grunt Versions

Grunt is constantly evolving, and you may decide you want your plug-in to support a minimum version of Grunt. The peerDepencencies key lets you do just that:

```
"peerDependencies": {
  "grunt": "~0.4.2"
}
```

This specifies that this plug-in will work with Grunt 0.4.2 and up, but not Grunt 0.5.0.

First, we install the grunt-contrib-jshint plug-in:

```
$ npm install grunt-contrib-jshint --save-dev
```

Next, we create a file called .jshintrc, which contains the rules we want to test our code against. We'll use the rules that other Grunt plug-ins use. Place the following lines of code in the file—you don't have to type in the comments for this to work, but you may want them anyway so you don't forget what these options do:

grunt-open-with-chrome/.jshintrc
```
{
  "node": true,      // For NodeJS
  "undef": true,     // Require all non-global variables to be declared
  "curly": true,     // Require curly braces for blocks and scope
  "eqeqeq": true,    // Require "===" instead of "==" for equality
  "immed": true,     // Must wrap immediate invoked functions in parens
  "latedef": true,   // Must define functions and variables before use
  "newcap": true,    // Constructor functions must be capitalized
  "noarg": true,     // Don't allow 'arguments.caller' and 'arguments.callee'
  "sub": true,       // Allow '[]' even if dot notation could be used
  "boss": true,      // Allow assignments where comparisons might be expected
  "eqnull": true     // Allow use of '== null'
}
```

Then we set up the Grunt task for JSHint by including the NodeJS module and configuring its options:

grunt-open-with-chrome/Gruntfile.js
```
grunt.loadNpmTasks('grunt-contrib-jshint');
grunt.config("jshint", {
  all: [
    'Gruntfile.js',
    'tasks/**/*.js'
  ],
  options: {
    jshintrc: '.jshintrc',
  },
});
```

We're configuring this task to look at all of the JavaScript files within the task folder, no matter how many folders deep they are. This ensures we check the lib folder too. We also let it look at the Gruntfile itself.

And now we can run the following to check for errors.

```
$ grunt jshint
Running "jshint:all" (jshint) task
>> 3 files lint free.

Done, without errors.
```

Any errors or warnings found will stop Grunt from processing any other tasks, so this is a great tool to add into a final build process to ensure that you've fixed all of your code issues before deploying things to production.

What's Next?

We've built a fairly simple plug-in in this chapter. From here we can publish our plug-in to the npm repository so others can use it. Of course, you'll want to investigate how to write unit tests for the launching functionality before releasing a Grunt plug-in. Here are a few more things you may want to play with:

- Implement a version of this plug-in that opens the Firefox web browser either instead of Chrome or alongside Chrome.

- Look at the source code for one of the other plug-ins we used in this book and see if you can find ways to improve it; submit any changes to the maintainer.

- We didn't write any unit tests for our plug-in. Unit-testing JavaScript programs is beyond the scope of this book, but you might want to investigate the Jasmine and Nodeunit testing libraries.[2,3]

Next, let's look at using Grunt templates to create projects instead of doing all this configuration by hand.

---

2.   http://jasmine.github.io/
3.   https://github.com/caolan/nodeunit

CHAPTER 6

Create Project Scaffolds

When you decide to work on a new project, you've got this great idea in your head and you can't wait to turn it into code. But sometimes the monotony of setting up folders, configuration files, and other required bits can slow your momentum considerably. Modern web projects have a ton of tooling that needs to be set up. For example, if you're going to use Grunt you'll need a package.json() file for your project, and you'll want a Gruntfile.js with your tasks already configured. And if you're doing any kind of unit testing you'll want your setup files for your test suite. You may even want to include JavaScript libraries. We can define our own project templates that give us just what we need.

The grunt-init command gives us the power to create new projects with ease. In Chapter 1, *The Very Basics*, on page 1, you learned about the npm init command that walks you through creating a new package.json file for your project. The grunt-init command uses a similar wizard-based system to help you create your own projects from templates. These templates can be distributed as plug-ins via npm, but these templates can also just be folders on your hard drive. In this chapter we'll look at an existing template and then we'll build our own template from scratch, which you can then modify to meet your own needs.

Before we begin, we need to install the grunt-init with npm globally so it's available everywhere on our systems. We do that through npm like this:

```
$ npm install -g grunt-init
```

Test it out by typing this:

```
$ grunt-init
```

It should report that no templates are found. That's expected, as we don't have any system-wide templates created.

Using Existing Templates

You install templates into a folder in your home folder. This will be ~/.grunt_init/ on OS X and Linux, and %USERPROFILE%\.grunt-init\ on Windows. Typically, since these templates are often located on GitHub, you'll use Git to clone the template into that folder. If you don't have the Git client installed, you can get installers for your operating system at the Git website.[1]

Let's clone the grunt-init-grunt template, which makes creating a new Gruntfile easy. First, we clone the template file to our machine's ~/.grunt-init/ folder. Open a new Terminal and ensure that you're in your home folder. Then use Git to clone the grunt-init-gruntfile plug-in into the folder .grunt-init/gruntfile within your home folder:

```
$ git clone https://github.com/gruntjs/grunt-init-gruntfile.git \
.grunt-init/gruntfile
```

And now we can try it out. When we run the template we'll be asked a series of questions, very similar to the ones we get when we use the npm init command. Our answers to the questions determine the values that end up in the Gruntfile and package.json file for the project.

```
$ grunt-init gruntfile
Running "init:gruntfile" (init) task
This task will create one or more files in the current directory, based on the
environment and the answers to a few questions. Note that answering "?" to any
question will show question-specific help and answering "none" to most questions
will leave their values blank.

"gruntfile" template notes:
This template tries to guess file and directory paths, but you will most likely
need to edit the generated Gruntfile.js file before running grunt. If you run
grunt after generating the Gruntfile, and it exits with errors, edit the file!

Please answer the following:
[?] Is the DOM involved in ANY way? (Y/n) n
[?] Will files be concatenated or minified? (Y/n) n
[?] Will you have a package.json file? (Y/n) y
[?] Do you need to make any changes to the above before continuing? (y/N) n

Writing Gruntfile.js...OK
Writing package.json...OK

Initialized from template "gruntfile".

Done, without errors.
```

---

1. http://git-scm.com/downloads

We can write our own questions and use those answers to include, exclude, and alter the content of new files. So let's dig in to creating our own template!

Creating a Custom Template

Let's create a template that sets up a basic HTML5 website with a single JavaScript file and a single stylesheet. We'll also add in a couple of additional prompts that let users decide if they'd like a Gruntfile, and if they'd like some default content added to the stylesheet. Our project will utilize the values the users provide in the JavaScript and the HTML content, too.

A template consists of a file called template.js that contains the main script executed by grunt-init, and a folder called root that contains the files that will make up the project. This root folder can have HTML files, JavaScript files, images, and pretty much anything else you think you might find useful. The following figure shows how the process will work:

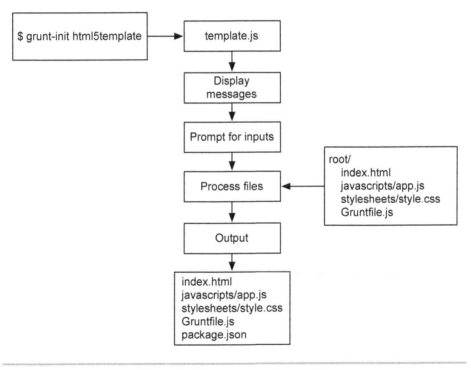

Figure 3—How our template works

Navigate to the .grunt-init folder in your home folder. Create a new folder called html5template within the .grunt-init. Then, inside this new folder, create a folder called root, which will contain all of the source files for our template:

```
$ cd .grunt-init
$ mkdir html5template
$ cd html5template
$ mkdir root
```

Next, create the template.js file. This is where the logic for our script will go. We'll use this file to define the questions we'll ask the user, along with the default answers, and we'll determine exactly how to process the template. We'll start out by defining a description of the template on the screen, along with some notes.

scaffolding/html5template/template.js
```
exports.description = 'Creates an HTML5 template with CSS and ' +
                      'JavaScript files.';

exports.notes = 'This project includes a default JavaScript and CSS file' +
                'In addition, you can choose to include an optional ' +
                'Gruntfile and some default CSS styles';
```

The description is displayed when you type the command grunt-init without any arguments. This command lists all the installed templates and their descriptions. The notes get displayed when you actually run the template.

The template itself is a basic function that takes in a grunt object, plus an init object and the done object that is used for asynchronous processing. We'll talk about how that works in Chapter 3, *One Task, Many Outputs*, on page 21.

```
exports.template = function(grunt, init, done) {
};
```

Inside of that function, we execute the init.process() method, which takes an options object, an array of input prompts, and a callback function that does the actual processing. Our template is very basic, so we'll pass in a blank options object. We'll also define an empty array of prompts, which we'll fill in shortly.

```
init.process({}, [
  // input prompts go here

], function(err, props) {
  // processing section
});
```

Now, let's look at how we can ask the user for input.

Prompting for Input

The input object has a prompt() function that defines a request for information from the user. There are many built-in ones, including the project's name, the project's author, the main starting point of the app, and even an open source library.

Inside of the empty array we created when we defined the init.process() function, add these lines:

```
// input prompts go here

// Prompt for these values.
init.prompt('name'  , 'AwesomeCo'),
init.prompt('author', 'Max Power'),
```

We're prompting for the name, the author, and the main file for the project. We can specify the default values for each of these as well.

Using Variables in Templates

The variables for the name and author are available in every file in the root folder. All we have to do is embed the values like this:

```
{%= name %}
```

So, let's create the template for the HTML page. In the root/index.html file, add this content:

```
scaffolding/html5template/root/index.html
<!DOCTYPE html>
<html lang="en-US">
  <head>
    <meta charset="utf-8">
➤   <title>{%= name %}</title>
    <link rel="stylesheet" href="stylesheets/app.css">
  </head>
  <body>
    <header>
➤     <h1>{%= name %}</h1>
    </header>
    <section>
      <p>Your content goes here.</p>
    </section>
    <footer>
➤     <small>Copyright {%= grunt.template.today('yyyy') %} {%= author %}</small>
    </footer>
    <script src="javascripts/app.js"></script>
  </body>
</html>
```

The highlighted sections show how we're using the name and author data we'll prompt users for when they run this template.

Look at this line:

```
scaffolding/html5template/root/index.html
<small>Copyright {%= grunt.template.today('yyyy') %} {%= author %}</small>
```

Grunt provides some special methods designed for use in templates. We can easily inject the current year into our template with grunt.template.date(). Passing in "yyyy" gives us the four-digit year.

Let's do something similar with our JavaScript file. Create a root/javascripts/app.js file with this content:

```
scaffolding/html5template/root/javascripts/app.js
/*
 * {%= name %}
 */
var app = {};
app.name = '{%= name %}';
```

We can use the input data in JavaScript code, too. Here we embed the name of the project as a name property of an app object.

No web project would be complete without a stylesheet, so let's add one. Create a stylesheets folder inside of the root folder:

```
$ mkdir root/stylesheets
```

Then create a stylesheet called app.css in that folder. We'll put in a simple rule that removes the default margin and padding from the body element:

```
scaffolding/html5template/root/stylesheets/app.css
body{
  margin: 0;
  padding: 0;
}
```

Any file or folder we put inside our template's root folder will get copied into the destination location, and so we could add more default stylesheets or scripts, like the Bootstrap framework, jQuery Mobile, or even something custom built.

Processing the Template

With the template files in place, we can turn our attention to the callback function in template.js. Add these lines to the body of the callback function of init.process():

```
var files = init.filesToCopy(props);
init.copyAndProcess(files, props);

init.writePackageJSON('package.json', props);

done();
```

First, we get the list of files we're going to process. This puts into an array the paths of all the files in the root folder and its child folders. Then we use the init.copyAndProcess() function to copy all the files and process their contents. The properties we set get passed along to this function and get used in the views.

Finally, the package.json file gets written, using the properties we prompted for.

Let's run this and see how it works. In a new Terminal, create a new folder called test, navigate into that folder, and run the grunt-init command with our template's name:

```
$ mkdir test
$ cd test
$ grunt-init html5template
Running "init:html5template/" (init) task
This task will create one or more files in the current directory,
based on the environment and the answers to a few questions. Note
that answering "?" to any question will show question-specific
help and answering "none" to most questions will leave their values
blank.

"html5template" template notes:
This project includes a default JavaScript and CSS file. In
addition, you can choose to include an optional Gruntfile and some
default CSS styles.

Please answer the following:
[?] Project name (AwesomeCo)
[?] author (Max Power)
[?] Main module/entry point (index.html)
[?] Do you need to make any changes to the above before
continuing? (y/N)

Writing index.html...OK
Writing javascripts/app.js...OK
Writing stylesheets/app.css...OK
Writing package.json...OK

Initialized from template "html5template".

Done, without errors.
```

And now when you look at the contents of the current folder, you'll see the generated files. The HTML file will contain values where the variables were. Let's take this a step further and see how we can skip files based on user input.

Including Files Conditionally

So far we've used the built-in prompts, but it might be nice if we let the users decide if they want us to generate a Gruntfile for their projects. We'll assume they do by default, but we'll give them the option to exclude it. We can do that with a custom prompt and a custom property.

First, ensure you're back in the html5template folder that contains your template files. Then add the file Gruntfile.js to the root folder that contains the following code:

```
scaffolding/html5template/root/Gruntfile.js
module.exports = function(grunt){
  grunt.initConfig({
    pkg: grunt.file.readJSON('package.json')
  });
}
```

This sample Gruntfile loads the package.json file into the variable pkg. It's a handy way to avoid repeating ourselves; we can now easily use the data in the package.json file inside of a Gruntfile. (We used this back in *Using Values from Files*, on page 18.) Since this is such a common practice, we want this in our template's Gruntfile.

Next, in template.js, in the prompts array, after the prompt for the name, author, and main file, add the following code to ask users if they'd like a Gruntfile:

```
scaffolding/html5template/template.js
{
  name: 'gruntfile',
  message: 'Do you want a Gruntfile?',
  default: 'Y/n',
  warning: 'If you want to be able to do cool stuff you should have one.'
},
```

This is an example of a custom prompt. We use a JavaScript object that contains the name, the prompt's message, the default value, and a warning message that is displayed to users if they don't choose a valid option.

We've asked for the value, so now let's use it. In the processing callback function, we'll need to turn the "yes" or "no" value the user entered into a Boolean. So, above the init.copyAndProcess() line, add this line:

```
props.gruntfile = /y/i.test(props.gruntfile);
```

Then right beneath that, add the logic to evaluate that variable, which is just a JavaScript if statement:

```
var files = init.filesToCopy(props);
if(props.gruntfile){
  props.devDependencies = {
    'grunt': '~0.4.4'
  };
}else{
  delete files['Gruntfile.js'];
}
```

If the user wants a Gruntfile, we make sure we add Grunt as a dependency to the package.json file. If he doesn't want a Gruntfile, then we remove the Gruntfile from the list of files we're going to copy. We always put every file possible into the template's root folder, and then we filter out what we don't want to copy.

Now when we run the command, we'll get the new prompt. If we answer yes, we'll get the Gruntfile, and Grunt gets added to our package.json file as a development dependency.

We can include or exclude files, but we can also include or exclude parts of our template files using a similar approach.

Including File Contents Conditionally

Using a custom prompt and some logic in the template.js file, we've been able to conditionally include or exclude a file from our template's root folder. But we can also use conditional logic in our template files.

The CSS property box-sizing: border-box is becoming quite popular. By default, an element's width equals the actual width of the element plus the margin, padding, and borders. That can make it really tricky to do math. But with border-box, an element's width is the defined width, and the padding, margins, and border do not affect the width. This makes doing columns a lot easier. However, it's not supported everywhere. So let's add a prompt to our configuration to let users decide if they want to use this rule. Add this new prompt to the template.js file, right below the prompt for the Gruntfile:

scaffolding/html5template/template.js

```
{
  name: 'gruntfile',
  message: 'Do you want a Gruntfile?',
  default: 'Y/n',
  warning: 'If you want to be able to do cool stuff you should have one.'
},
```

```
➤ {
➤   name: 'borderbox',
➤   message: 'Do you want to use the border-box styling in CSS?',
➤   default: 'Y/n'
➤ },
```

Then, in the processing section, below the property evaluation for the Gruntfile, add this line to handle the border-box property:

```
  props.gruntfile = /y/i.test(props.gruntfile);
➤ props.borderbox = /y/i.test(props.borderbox);
```

Finally, add the following code to root/stylesheets/app.css:

```
scaffolding/html5template/root/stylesheets/app.css
body{
  margin: 0;
  padding: 0;
}
{% if (borderbox) {%}
/* apply a natural box layout model to all elements
 * http://www.paulirish.com/2012/box-sizing-border-box-ftw/
 */
*, *:before, *:after {
  -webkit-box-sizing: border-box;
     -moz-box-sizing: border-box;
          box-sizing: border-box;

}
{% } %}
```

Our definition for border-box is wrapped in an if statement; it'll be written only if the user sets the property! It's that easy to do conditional content. Just watch out for the syntax of the if statement here—it's very easy to forget one of the curly braces.

Running grunt-init html5template again now results in this additional question, and if we answer yes, our CSS file will have the border-box code. If we answer no, our CSS file will be blank.

What's Next?

Grunt templates are incredibly powerful if you do a lot of new-project work. They can be a great way to bootstrap a project of any type, too. You could use them to generate a project in any language, for any reason you see fit. And you can share your templates with the world. Before moving on, though, explore these additional topics:

The rename.json File

The file rename.json lets you map files in your template's root directory to destination locations. You can even change the names of the files using template strings. Here's an example from the grunt-init-jquery plug-in:

```
{
  "src/name.js": "src/jquery.{%= name %}.js",
  "test/name_test.js": "test/{%= name %}_test.js",
  "test/name.html": "test/{%= name %}.html"
}
```

You could specify a completely different destination folder, which might let you better organize the files in your template.

- Right now, files that exist are automatically overwritten when we run the template again. The exports.warnOn property lets us specify a pattern of files that should not be overwritten. If the template runner encounters any files in the current folder that match this pattern, it will abort the script. Add this into the script at the top to prevent overwriting any file.

- Modify the template so that the object in the JavaScript file is included only if the user requests it. Make a new prompt and a new property, and then optionally include the source code.

- Include a README.md file in Markdown format in the project that specifies the project name and description. Create a new prompt that asks for the project description to populate the value.

- Modify the template so that it optionally includes support for Sass and CoffeeScript based on user prompts. Use the Grunt configuration you built in Chapter 4, *Build a Workflow*, on page 31, as your guide. As an extra step, if the plug-in uses CoffeeScript, include a CoffeeScript file instead of the JavaScript file. If the user requests Sass, include a Sass file instead of the CSS file. Remember to alter the watch() task so that it invokes the tasks to compile CoffeeScript or Sass files.

At this point you should feel much more comfortable with how Grunt works. Look at the projects you maintain and investigate how Grunt can improve your development and deployment workflow. Use the multitude of well-tested plug-ins available, but don't be afraid to create your own templates and plug-ins whenever it makes sense.

From here, you might want to look at other projects, such as Yeoman, which is a project generator that relies on Grunt. Yeoman makes it a snap to create modern web projects.[2] Another great option is Lineman, which provides a thin wrapper around Grunt, creating an awesome workflow for client-side web applications.[3] You'll find those projects easy to use with your newfound understanding of Grunt.

```
$ grunt automate:everything
```

---

2.   http://yeoman.io/
3.   http://linemanjs.com/

Bibliography

[Bur11]   Trevor Burnham. *CoffeeScript: Accelerated JavaScript Development*. The
          Pragmatic Bookshelf, Raleigh, NC and Dallas, TX, 2011.

[CC11]   Hampton Catlin and Michael Lintorn Catlin. *Pragmatic Guide to Sass*. The
          Pragmatic Bookshelf, Raleigh, NC and Dallas, TX, 2011.

Long Live the Command Line!

Use tmux and Vim for incredible mouse-free productivity.

tmux

Your mouse is slowing you down. The time you spend context switching between your editor and your consoles eats away at your productivity. Take control of your environment with tmux, a terminal multiplexer that you can tailor to your workflow. Learn how to customize, script, and leverage tmux's unique abilities and keep your fingers on your keyboard's home row.

Brian P. Hogan
(88 pages) ISBN: 9781934356968. $16.25
http://pragprog.com/book/bhtmux

Practical Vim

Vim is a fast and efficient text editor that will make you a faster and more efficient developer. It's available on almost every OS—if you master the techniques in this book, you'll never need another text editor. In more than 100 Vim tips, you'll quickly learn the editor's core functionality and tackle your trickiest editing and writing tasks.

Drew Neil
(346 pages) ISBN: 9781934356982. $29
http://pragprog.com/book/dnvim

The Pragmatic Bookshelf

The Pragmatic Bookshelf features books written by developers for developers. The titles continue the well-known Pragmatic Programmer style and continue to garner awards and rave reviews. As development gets more and more difficult, the Pragmatic Programmers will be there with more titles and products to help you stay on top of your game.

Visit Us Online

This Book's Home Page
http://pragprog.com/book/bhgrunt
Source code from this book, errata, and other resources. Come give us feedback, too!

Register for Updates
http://pragprog.com/updates
Be notified when updates and new books become available.

Join the Community
http://pragprog.com/community
Read our weblogs, join our online discussions, participate in our mailing list, interact with our wiki, and benefit from the experience of other Pragmatic Programmers.

New and Noteworthy
http://pragprog.com/news
Check out the latest pragmatic developments, new titles and other offerings.

Save on the eBook

Save on the eBook versions of this title. Owning the paper version of this book entitles you to purchase the electronic versions at a terrific discount.

PDFs are great for carrying around on your laptop—they are hyperlinked, have color, and are fully searchable. Most titles are also available for the iPhone and iPod touch, Amazon Kindle, and other popular e-book readers.

Buy now at *http://pragprog.com/coupon*

Contact Us

Online Orders:	*http://pragprog.com/catalog*
Customer Service:	*support@pragprog.com*
International Rights:	*translations@pragprog.com*
Academic Use:	*academic@pragprog.com*
Write for Us:	*http://pragprog.com/write-for-us*
Or Call:	+1 800-699-7764

CPSIA information can be obtained at www.ICGtesting.com
Printed in the USA
BVOW10s1408160614

356487BV00001B/1/P